Tolerance Tykes:

Teaching Tools For A Better Tomorrow

Written and Illustrated by Brooke Aiello

Copyright © 2017 by Brooke Aiello
www.ToleranceTykes.com

All rights reserved. No part of this book may be reproduced by any means without written permission of
the publisher.

Library of Congress Control Number: 2017913367
ISBN 978-0-692-93709-9

Published by Tolerant Tidings, LLC Glastonbury, CT USA
November 2017

This Book Belongs to:

_____

3

A Letter to Parents, Teachers, and Caregivers

Tolerance Tykes first came to fruition after writing a poem about my observations growing up. It seemed that everywhere I turned, children were afraid to be themselves for fear of what others may think. There was never a book I came across that showed the feelings of children facing challenges from their point of view. *Tolerance Tykes* began with one poem I wrote for a young girl struggling with Gender Identity Disorder. When her mother expressed what a positive effect it had on her daughter's self-confidence, I knew this was a project I had to pursue. I decided to continue the series by adding children from different walks of life to fill the classroom in my book. One by one, my characters came to life, poem after poem, and illustration after illustration. I found my greatest inspiration in the lives of people I know and love, like my best friend Morgan!

Children who are different often experience bullying. Bullying starts at a young age due to ignorance towards the unknown. *Tolerance Tykes* was designed to get to the root of the problem and educate children on the issues, rather than try to heal wounds once the bullying has started. Each year, new students, each unique in their own way, will join Miss Brooke's classroom. The goal is to provide the reader with a firsthand look at what a child they may not initially relate to is going through. Each character in the book has their very own poem, followed by a short lesson and discussion you can have with your child or student.

Not only is bullying detrimental to a child's education, development, and self-confidence, but its effects follow long past adolescence. As adults, it is easy to look at the world we live in and realize the ignorance and intolerance is a learned epidemic. Please join me on this journey in teaching children and adults alike that everyone deserves to be happy, loved, and proud of who they are. When we can look beyond what makes us different, we will realize that we all have something in common. Each one of us, regardless of our age, gender, race, religion, or abilities is a human being who deserves to get the best out of the life they were given.

-Brooke Aiello

4

What is Tolerance Tykes?

Tolerance Tykes was created to promote the inclusivity of children from all walks of life.

My hopes as the author and illustrator are to break down walls of intolerance that stand in the way of compassion and kindness.

Whether this book is on a shelf at home, school, or your local library, I hope that it instills a message to each child it reaches that they are beautiful and important just the way they are.

Meet the Class

Meet Chrissy

I Am Transgender
Page 16

Meet Paul

I Have Autism
Page 20

Meet Hope

I Have Anxiety
Page 24

Meet Danny

I Have Down Syndrome
Page 28

Meet Paige

I Have Muscular Dystrophy

Page 32

Meet Morgan

I Have Cancer

Page 36

Meet Brett

I Am Deaf

Page 40

Meet William

I Am Adopted

Page 44

Meet Sarah

I Have A Stutter

Page 48

Meet Zane

I Am Blind

Page 52

Meet Miss Brooke

I'm The Author & Illustrator

Brooke Aiello is the sole creator of *Tolerance Tykes: Teaching Tools for a Better Tomorrow.* As the author and illustrator, Brooke has dedicated countless hours to create a series that gives a voice to children who are oftentimes not heard. Using personal experience, experiences from people she loves, and a passion for poetry and art, she proudly introduces her classroom. Her hope is to spread kindness, knowledge, and tolerance to those her stories may reach. When not writing and illustrating, this lifelong Connecticut resident can be found spending time with those she loves the most.

Hello, boys and girls! It's a pleasure to meet you!
My name is Miss Brooke; it's an honor to teach you.
Where do I begin in explaining to you,
How lucky I am to teach the lessons I do.

The children in my classroom are one of a kind,
And I handcraft each lesson with them in mind.
Each seat in the room, I proudly fill,
With special young children like Chrissy and Will.

Each and every morning, when roll call is done,
We quickly get to business and start having fun!
I plan out each lesson with one goal in mind,
To create a world that's beautiful, accepting, and kind.

It's not our job to change what we see,
You are you and I am me,
Accepting one another is the name of the game,
When it comes to a world where we aren't all the same.

Please join me as I round up
the troops,
And introduce you to the most
special of groups.
You'll quickly learn what each of
them likes,
I proudly present my Tolerance
Tykes.

In the first row, we have Chrissy and Paul,
Chrissy is playful and Paul's off the wall.
Paul has autism and learns a different way.
His wonderful smile brightens my day.

Chrissy is beautiful; I'll always defend her,
You see, Chrissy was born with the opposite gender.

Right behind Chrissy is sweet little Hope,
She suffers from anxiety, but we all help her cope.

The next row over sits Danny and Paige,
Danny has Down syndrome; he's nine years of age.

When describing Danny,
don't use the word down,
He's the exact opposite;
he's our class clown.

Paige has a wheelchair
with bright pink wheels,
She speeds fast at recess
and likes how it feels.

Front and center across from my chair,
Sits little Morgan who's losing her hair.

Morgan has cancer, she's had it awhile,
But you'll never see Morgan without a big smile.

Right next to Morgan is
sweet little Brett,
He's the kindest little boy
you have ever met.

He is sweet to everyone
and his kindness lingers,
But he says no words,
he signs with his fingers.

William is one of my favorite lads,
He is very proud of having
two dads.
He happily states that
his fathers are gay,
He wouldn't want them
any other way.

Right behind William,
sits a friend who's more shy,
She has trouble with words,
but will always try.

Sarah has a stutter, but none
of us mind,
We help her find her voice
and it's always so kind.

Sarah's best friend is sweet little Zane,
He's not able to see and walks with a cane.

He is joined in school by
his guide dog, Jack,
Who sits quietly next
to Zane's backpack.

I can't wait for you to join us at school,
Where we will teach you that different is cool.

You're always welcome
the way you are,
In this
beautiful planet,
you're a bright
shining star.

If you feel different, please have no fear,
Pull up a seat, you're always safe here.

Meet Chrissy

I Am Transgender

Like Mommy, Like Me

My name is Christopher, but Chrissy to me.
That name goes better with who I want to be.
My father's a tough guy, tall and strong,
My mom is beautiful with hair blonde and long.
Dad tells mom she's pretty, believe me it's true.
Someday I'd like to feel pretty too.

I know what you're thinking, pretty is for girls,
The dresses, the make-up, and those awesome fake pearls.
But I can be pretty, at least in my heart,
I have to tell mom, but where can I start?

Mommy, please listen, I'll try to explain,
I don't feel like a boy inside of my brain.
I don't fit in with the neighborhood boys,
But the girls are real fun and I love their toys.

After I told her, I was really surprised,
She told me she loved me with tears in her eyes.
"I've held you, I've raised you, and I've watched you grow,
Thank you for telling me, but I already know."

"Chrissy, is it? I like that name too!
I'll call you that now if you want me to.
It may not be easy as time goes by,
But we've talked to a doctor and we sure will try."

I just can't believe it, my dreams will come true,
Not just mine, but people like me too.
My doctor told me not to be sad,
Between my body and brains, the matching was bad.

He said as I grow up, my body can be fixed,
That must be one of those doctor tricks.
"You'll be Chrissy in no time," the doctor did add,
"You have a lovely young daughter," he said to my dad.

To everyone out there who feels the same way:

"I promise that you will be happy someday.
Just believe in yourself, despite the world,
And know that you're special,"
Love, this brave little girl.

Chrissy's Comments

Hi, everyone! Thanks for stopping by! I wanted to go over what you may have learned after reading "Like Mommy, Like Me". I am transgender! Being transgender means that the gender I feel on the inside does not match the body I have on the outside. When I was born, everyone yelled, "It's a boy!" because of how I looked. I knew when I was very little that I was meant to be a girl, even though I was born a boy. Being transgender can be hard sometimes because most people do not understand how it feels. I am so lucky that my family, friends, and Miss Brooke support me. There is nothing like being who you are! For more learning, fun, and activities with me, be sure to check out my page on ToleranceTykes.com.

Chrissy

How Should You Treat Someone Who Is Transgender?

• **BE KIND:** Even though you might not understand what it feels like to be transgender, it is important to always be kind. Be sure to always call that person by the name they choose to go by. It is also important to use the pronouns they identify with, like he, she, they, or them.

• **STAND UP:** If you see someone being bullied because they are transgender, stand up for them and let others know that bullying is not ok.

• **LEARN:** Get to know someone who is transgender and learn all about what it is like to be them. Not only will you learn a lot about someone who is different than you, but you also might make a new friend.

• **TEACH:** If you or someone you know is transgender, teach others what it means. Spread kindness and teach anyone you can how to treat people who are different than you.

• **UNDERSTAND:** Being transgender can be difficult for people at times, especially because some people don't understand what it means. Work to understand what a transgender person might feel, and think about things from their point of view..

• **SUPPORT:** If you know someone who is transgender, like Chrissy, be supportive and let them know that you are there for them. Feeling different is hard, and we can all give our support so everyone feels included and special.

Homework

Let's Chat!

1) How would you treat a child like Chrissy?

2) Do you know anyone who is transgender?

3) It's ok to ask questions! What would you ask a transgender person?

Look It Up!
How many people in the United States identify as transgender?

Meet Paul

I Have Autism

Paul's Piece of the Puzzle

My name is Paul; I'm in grade three,
I like running, dancing, or climbing a tree.
One minute I'm laughing, the next I'm upset.
Can you tell that I have autism yet?

Autism controls how I live each day,
I may lose control or go the opposite way.
I try my hardest to fit in with the crowd,
But the noises in life are sometimes too loud.

I'm easily triggered by something I see,
And my disability then takes hold of me.
I don't want to act up, trust me, it's true,
But sometimes I'm lost and don't know what to do.

I'm too hyper to sleep, too distracted to eat,
I get stuck on my words and tap both of my feet.
I get lost in my thoughts, and I sometimes just cry.
I may not fit in, but I do always try.

My third-grade classroom is my favorite place.
They don't judge disabilities, gender, or race.
I can run wild at recess with no regrets.
Being different is something the whole class gets.

My best friend is Danny, his syndrome is Down's,
He can turn around even the saddest of frowns.
The spectrum disorder I live with each day,
Doesn't change how he sees me in any way.

Thank you for listening, I'm off to school,
Where kindness is always the number one rule.
Autism is something I can't always control,
But doing my best is always my goal.

Paul's Points

Hi! I hope you enjoyed reading "Paul's Piece of the Puzzle".
I'm Paul and I have autism. Being on the autism
spectrum means that my brain has developed
differently than other children I know. Sometimes
I have a hard time listening, talking, playing, and
learning. Autism is a spectrum disorder, meaning
that it can affect everyone differently. You may not always know what
I'm thinking or doing, but please always be kind. It can be very
frustrating not having control over how I feel. For more learning, fun,
and activities with me, head on over to my
page on ToleranceTykes.com.

PAUL

How Should You Treat Someone Who Has Autism?

• **BE KIND:** Everyone's brain works differently, whether someone is on the autism spectrum or not. It is important to accept everyone for who they are and be patient and kind when someone is different than you.

• **STAND UP:** If you see someone being bullied because they are on the autism spectrum, stand up for them and let other people know that bullying is not ok.

• **LEARN:** Get to know someone who is on the autism spectrum and learn all about what it is like to be them. Not only will you learn about someone that may be different than you, but you could also make a new friend!

• **TEACH:** If you or someone you know is on the autism spectrum, take time to teach other people what having autism means. The more people who know about autism, the less likely they are to bully someone who is on the spectrum.

• **UNDERSTAND:** Being on the autism spectrum can make everyday activities harder. Being in large crowds, sitting still in class, and communicating with people are a few ways in which people with autism may struggle. It is important to understand that people on the autism spectrum are no different than anyone else, besides the fact that they may learn and communicate differently.

• **SUPPORT:** If you know someone who has autism, like Paul, be as supportive as possible. Let them know that you are there for them. Feeling different is hard, but the more we know and support one another, the less different we become.

Homework

Let's Chat!

1) Do you know anyone on the autism spectrum?

2) How would you help Paul feel like everyone else in class?

3) What activities could you do with someone who has autism?

Look It Up!
Find a famous celebrity who is on the autism spectrum!

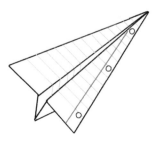

Meet Hope

I Have Anxiety

Hope You Feel Better

Hello, everyone, the pleasure is all mine.
I'm in the third grade and I just turned nine.
I have anxiety disorder and sometimes can't cope.
I forgot to mention, my name is Hope.

Anxiety has symptoms that most people can't see.
I carry these symptoms all day with me.
I oftentimes worry about things I can't change,
And when I have these symptoms, I may act strange.

Anxiety can show up any time of the day.
When I'm feeling anxious, I may not say.
You might think I'm being shy, or I'm angry with you,
But sometimes being alone is all I can do.

I try my best to be as perfect as can be,
And make sure my family is proud of me.
I put a lot of pressure on myself day by day,
When it comes to my grades and the sports that I play.

The kids I go to school with all know how I feel,
And though they can't see it, anxiety is real.
When I start to feel anxious over a field trip or test,
They all love and support me, my friends are the best.

Miss Brooke, my teacher, has anxiety as well.
And whenever I'm worrying, she can always tell.
She tells me to breathe and I take a quick walk,
Then return to the classroom so we can talk.

Anxiety is something that you can't always express,
But it causes me to panic, and it fills me with stress.
It's something that I have to work on to fix.
So I practice my breathing and other neat tricks.

I don't mean to seem rude, or angry, or sad,
But it comes out of nowhere and makes me feel bad.
I know from the outside, I look normal as can be,
But the symptoms I have, no one can see.

Anxiety is a disorder that many people may face,
It can affect any age, gender, or race.
Always be patient and always be kind,
Not all illnesses are visible, some start with your mind.

Hope's Hints

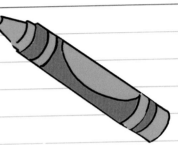

Hi, everyone! I am so glad you got to read, "Hope you Feel Better"! My name is Hope and I have anxiety! Anxiety is something I cannot control, and it all starts with a small thought in my brain.

If something upsets me or causes me to worry, that small thought grows and grows until I cannot control how it makes me feel. Anxiety is very common and can affect people of any age. Many people know what it feels like to have anxiety. For more learning, fun, and activities with me, click the link on my page at ToleranceTykes.com.

How Should You Treat Someone Who Has Anxiety?

• **BE KIND:** Always be kind to people no matter what they are going through. Anxiety is something that can come out of nowhere and affect how a person lives. No one should feel badly about having anxiety because it is not something they choose to have.

• **STAND UP:** If you see someone you know who has anxiety and is being bullied, stand up for them and let everyone know that bullying is not ok.

• **LEARN:** Get to know someone who has anxiety and take the time to learn how you can help them handle their feelings.

• **TEACH:** If you or someone you know has anxiety, teach others what you know. The more people who know what it is like to have anxiety, the more people who will be able to share their support.

• **UNDERSTAND:** Understand that anxiety can be a scary feeling. Do your best to be patient with someone who may be anxious. It's ok if someone does not want to share what is bothering them, but try your best to let them know that they will be ok and that you're there for them.

• **SUPPORT:** If you know anyone dealing with anxiety, like Hope, find out how you can help them when they are feeling anxious. Be patient, and learn breathing exercises and other activities that can take their mind off the anxiety.

Homework

Let's Chat!

1) How would you help someone with anxiety?

2) Do you or someone you know have anxiety disorder?

3) What are some things people may have anxiety about and why?

Look It Up!
How many children in the United States are affected by anxiety?

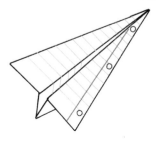

Meet Danny

I Have Down Syndrome

Danny's Day

Hello, my name is Danny; I am nine years old.
March 21st is my day, or so I have been told.
You see, I have Down syndrome, and I love to have fun!
Let's celebrate my difference in Chromosome 21.

Chromosomes tell your body the traits that will show,
Your eye and hair color, and how tall you'll grow.
Most people, you see, have twenty-three sets,
But I'm blessed with one more than everyone else gets.

Down syndrome is genetic; I've had it since birth,
But that doesn't take away from my worth.
I may look different, but please always be nice,
It's not my fault I got some chromosomes twice.

I may look different than the kids in your school,
But in mine, we're all different, but different is cool.
We all work together to let everyone see,
Everyone is special, as special can be.

Next week is my party; I just have seven more days.
We will learn about Down syndrome in so many ways!
My mom will make cupcakes or some healthy treat,
I can feel the excitement from my nose to my feet.

My teacher, Miss Brooke, is good at this stuff. She makes people feel special when life gets tough.
The kids in my classroom all feel the same way. In fact, each one of us has our own special day!

Chrissy has her party in the month of November. Transgender Day is always one to remember!
I learned not to judge her for her favorite toys. Things shouldn't be labeled for girls or for boys.

My best friend Paul's day is the month after mine!
Paul has autism and he just turned nine.
He may be really hyper and takes a little longer,
But the differences we share make our friendship much stronger.

Everyone deserves the chance to have a wedding,
It's ok to be gay! What are people not getting?
In June one year, they all signed a bill.
And we celebrated all day for the two dads of Will!

The rest of the year will be filled with great cheer.
We will celebrate Brett, who's not able to hear.
We will all sing for Morgan, when she finds the cure.
She is battling cancer, and we fight next to her.

We will all hold Hope's hand if she's feeling down,
I'll make her laugh; I'm her favorite class clown.
We will yell loud for Paige as she races the clock,
And support our friend Sarah through every speech block.
We will party with Zane, I'll write invites to mail,
Did I mention the invites were written in braille?

I'll never judge you for the way that you are,
In the big planet we live in, I love every star.
Be kind to everyone, and let them shine bright.
Share a smile with everyone each day and night.

29

Danny's Details

Hello! My name is Danny. Thank you so much for reading "Danny's Day". I am so proud to have Down syndrome because it makes me who I am. I have Down syndrome because I was born with an extra chromosome. People without Down syndrome have 46 chromosomes in their DNA. I am lucky enough to have one extra special chromosome, giving me 47! I may look and learn differently than you, but that's no reason to treat me differently than anyone else. Ask a parent, guardian, or teacher to help you look up more about what it's like to have Down syndrome and visit my page on ToleranceTykes.com for more fun and activities!

Danny

How Should You Treat Someone Who Has Down Syndrome?

• **BE KIND:** Everyone is different. It is important to remember to be kind to everyone who may look, learn, and develop differently than you.

• **STAND UP:** If you see someone being bullied because they have Down syndrome, stand up for them and let others know that bullying is not ok.

• **LEARN:** Take the time to get to know someone who has Down syndrome and learn what it is like to be them.

• **TEACH:** If you or someone you know has Down syndrome, teach others just how special that extra chromosome can make a person. The more people who know what it is like, the less likely they are to bully someone.

• **UNDERSTAND:** Understand that while having Down syndrome may make certain things hard, there is no reason that you shouldn't include someone with Down syndrome in fun activities. People with Down syndrome are some of the most loving people you could ever meet.

• **SUPPORT:** If you know someone who has Down syndrome, like Danny, let them know that you support them. Having support can make all the difference.

Homework

Let's Chat!

1) Do you or someone you know have Down syndrome?

2) How could you teach people about Down syndrome?

3) If you had a child like Danny in your class, how could you include them in fun activities?

Look It Up!

Can you find a model or actor who has Down syndrome?

Meet Paige

I Have Muscular Dystrophy

Racing for Kindness

Hi, everyone, my name is Paige.
I'm loving and smart and nine years of age.
There is more to me than the chair where I sit,
I'm not able to walk, have you noticed it?

I may not hop, skip, or run,
But wheels don't stop me from having fun.
I play tag at recess, basketball after school,
I love my wheelchair, it's different, it's cool.

I have Muscular Dystrophy, let me explain,
My muscles are weak and I'm sometimes in pain.
My body lacks proteins that help me grow strong,
And though I have energy, it doesn't last long.

It wasn't my choice to be this sick.
I can't run beside you, but my wheelchair is quick.
I hold the class record for fastest track laps,
I get the most cheers and the loudest claps.

My friends and my family are my biggest support,
In class, at home, or on the basketball court.
We all help each other be the best we can be,
That is what means the most to me.

My life isn't all winning races and fun,
I have doctor's appointments, one after one.
I depend on my family and friends for so much,
Like reaching high shelves, shopping and such.

The kids in my class are the best they can be,
They do everything they can to always help me.
Last year, four ramps were built in my name,
To make sure that everyone in town felt the same.

Please be kind, it's the number one rule,
Words can hurt and staring is cruel.
It isn't my choice to have this disease,
But I'm more than the disability that everyone sees.

Paige's Post

I'm Paige! I raced over here to check how you liked "Racing For Kindness", the story about what it's like having Muscular Dystrophy. Muscular Dystrophy is a disease that I was born with. My muscles do not get the right amount of proteins and it causes my muscles to get weaker and weaker. I may not be able to walk, but I have one of the coolest wheelchairs around. I love playing sports, going to school, and being with my friends and family. I don't let my wheelchair or my disability make me feel any less special than anyone else. Care to race? To check out more fun and activities with me, see my link on ToleranceTykes.com.

Paige

How Should You Treat Someone Who Has Muscular Dystrophy?

• **BE KIND:** Everyone's body works differently and these differences can make growing up hard. Be kind to people no matter how they get around each day.

• **STAND UP:** If you see someone being bullied because they have Muscular Dystrophy, stand up for them. Let others know that it is not ok to bully anyone because they are different.

• **LEARN:** Take the time to get to know someone who has Muscular Dystrophy and learn what it is like to be them.

• **TEACH:** If you or someone you know has Muscular Dystrophy, teach others what it is like. The more people who know about Muscular Dystrophy, the less likely they will be to bully someone.

• **UNDERSTAND:** Understand that even though Muscular Dystrophy may cause someone to not be able to participate in every activity, you should always make an effort to include them and let them decide if it's something they can or want to do.

• **SUPPORT:** If you know someone who has Muscular Dystrophy, like Paige, let them know that you support them. Support from others can make all the difference.

Homework

Let's Chat!

1) How would you treat Paige if she were in your class?

2) Do you know anyone with Muscular Dystrophy?

3) What are some fun activities that you could do with someone in a wheelchair?

Look It Up!

What is the name of the sporting event that allows people with physical disabilities to participate in over 20 sports across the world?

Meet Morgan

I Have Cancer

Three Cheers for Morgan

My name is Morgan; I'm in grade three. I'm spunky, loud, and cute as can be.
I like making people laugh with a joke or a trick, even though lately I've been feeling so sick.

When I was not feeling well, just two months ago,
My doctor told my parents there was something to know.
Cells help your body get well when you're sick, but my cells were growing and spreading too quick.

When my cells grew too fast and started to clump, it turned into a tumor, or a really big bump.
My mom thought I was allergic to one thing or two, I lost a lot of weight and had signs of the flu.

My doctor came into the room with a frown and told us the news when we all sat down.
The cancer I had was one you could treat, unlike some cancers that no one can beat.

In school on Monday, I thought I should share,
When I come back after treatment, I may not have hair.
I'll miss reading circle and a field trip or two, but that's what people with cancer must do.

My friends at school grabbed hold of my hand,
They'll miss me so much, but they all understand.
My teacher, Miss Brooke, gave me a big hug, and joined our class on the reading rug.

She helped answer questions for the kids in third grade,
To help them understand and not be afraid.
She sent home a letter to each parent that night,
Encouraging get-well notes with the address to write.

Two weeks at the hospital and I was feeling upset,
It was the day of a field trip, how could I forget.
The kids in my class all had the chance
To watch actors on a stage all sing and dance.

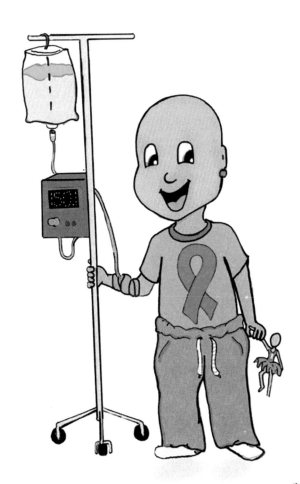

Just as a tear fell from my eye,
A knock on the door made me not cry.
One by one I saw the kids in my class,
Holding in their hands, a hospital pass.
They all were so sad that I was sick in my bed,
So they canceled the field trip to visit instead.

They said no field trip, no matter the place,
Would be more important than my smiling face.
I couldn't believe it; it was a dream come true!
Not only did they come, but the actors came too!

Six months after that, I had lost all of my hair,
But I was happy to be back in my classroom chair.
My friends threw a party and tied balloons to my seat,
To welcome me back from the cancer I'd beat.

If you don't understand what cancer might be,
Please read this story I wrote about me.
If you see someone with cancer, no matter their grade,
Please don't be mean, they're already afraid.

No matter the problem, or why someone's sick,
Great friends and a smile will help them heal quick.

Morgan's Mission

Hello, everyone, and thank you for coming to visit! "Three Cheers for Morgan" is the story about how I found out I had cancer. All living things have billions of cells that make up who they are. Unlike normal cells, cancerous cells grow and spread very quickly and make you feel sick. When I learned I had cancer, I went to a special doctor called an oncologist. They did everything they could to make me healthy again. Chemotherapy and radiation therapy are used to beat these cancerous cells. It is important to remember that cancer is not contagious, so don't be afraid to visit someone you know who has cancer. Being diagnosed with cancer was scary, and the love and support I got from my friends made me feel so much better. For more learning, fun, and activities, check out my page on ToleranceTykes.com.

Morgan

How Should You Treat Someone Who Has Cancer?

- **BE KIND:** Having an illness can be very difficult. It is important to always be kind no matter what someone is going through.

- **STAND UP:** If you see someone being bullied because they have cancer, stand up for them and let others know that bullying is not ok.

- **LEARN:** Get to know someone who has or has had cancer. Take the time to learn what it is like. You never know what you will learn.

- **TEACH:** If you or someone you know has cancer, teach others about what it is like. The more people who know the experience of someone with cancer, the less likely they will be to bully someone.

- **UNDERSTAND:** Understand that being diagnosed with cancer is hard. People who have cancer may be in and out of the hospital in order to get better. Some people who are battling cancer may lose their hair. Everyone has different things they struggle with.

- **SUPPORT:** If you know someone who has cancer, let them know that you support them. Having support during a hard time might be just what the doctor ordered.

Homework

Let's Chat!

1) How would you treat Morgan if she were a student in your class?

2) Do you know anyone who has cancer?

3) How could you show your support for people who are battling cancer?

Look It Up!

How many cancer survivors are there across the world?

Meet Brett

I Am Deaf

Send Me a Sign

My name is Brett; welcome to school,
Where being kind is our number one rule.
I'm in grade three, I'm almost nine,
My language of choice is always to sign.

I'm not able to hear, I haven't since birth,
But that's never taken away from my worth.
My family and friends all know sign language as well,
They love me so much and it's easy to tell.

In my classroom, the students are better than best,
My teacher, Miss Brooke, treats me just like the rest.
No matter what, we are all treated the same,
Kindness is always the name of the game.

I was born with some damage, deep in my ear,
I don't get the same signals as people who hear.
My eardrum may vibrate with every sound,
But the sound waves to my brain are never found.

Last week, my doctor gave my family a call,
I got approved for hearing aids, I get them this fall.
I cannot believe I will soon have the chance,
To hear crystal clear with cochlear implants.

The sound will soon travel from tunnel to drum,
And I will now hear where it's coming from.
The birds will be chirping, the thunder will roar,
I'll hear my mom yelling my name at the store.

My brother and sister will tell me their jokes,
I'll hear about work from my hardworking folks.
I'll hear lots of laughter and enjoy a good song,
It's finally happening, I've waited so long.

To the other people out there who have hearing loss too,
Please don't give up, whatever you do.
No matter what happens, you will always be fine,
If you ever need to talk, just send me a sign.

Brett's Bulletin Board

Hi, everyone! My name is Brett, and I am deaf! I hope you learned a lot about me after reading " Send Me a Sign". Being deaf means that one or more parts of my ear do not work, making it hard for me to hear without the help of hearing aids or surgery. I rely on the use of sign language to communicate with my friends and family. Being deaf can make it hard to communicate with people, but I am so happy that I have the support of my friends and family. For more learning, fun, and activities, check out my link on ToleranceTykes.com.

Brett

How Should You Treat Someone Who Is Deaf?

• **BE KIND:** Not being able to hear can make growing up hard. Remember, you can show kindness with actions and a smile.

• **STAND UP:** If you see someone you know being bullied because they are deaf, stand up for them and let everyone know that bullying is not ok.

• **LEARN:** Get to know someone who is deaf and take the time to learn about their experience. Finding new ways to communicate can be fun.

• **TEACH:** If you or someone you know is deaf, teach others what it is like. The more people who know, the less likely they will be to bully someone that is different than them.

• **UNDERSTAND:** Understand that even though being deaf can be hard, people who are deaf can do anything anyone else can do. Many people have hearing aids, and everyone's abilities are different.

• **SUPPORT:** If you know someone who is deaf, like Brett, let them know that you support them. Having support from friends can make all the difference to someone.

Homework

Let's Chat!

1) Do you know anyone who is deaf? Who?

2) If you went to school with a child like Brett, how would you help them feel included?

3) Do you know any sign language?

Look It Up!

Can you find three different forms of sign language? What are some similarities and differences among the different forms?

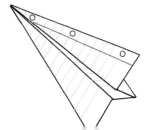

Meet William

I Am Adopted

All You Need Is Love

My name is William; I'm in grade three,
I'd like to tell you some facts about me.
I'm athletic and smart and one of a kind,
And have the very best dads a boy could find.

Many families begin with a husband and a wife,
But some families may lead a different life.
There's no right or wrong when it comes to the way
A child is cared for and loved each day.

My dads see every assignment and game-winning catch,
And they make sure my sneakers and t-shirts match.
We have family vacations and dinner each night,
And they teach me the difference between wrong and right.

Being a family means showing you love and support,
My family began with a judge in a court.
After being in foster care for as long as I can remember,
My fathers welcomed me home as a new family member.

I got my very own room in a house that's so cool,
I have a dog named Max and a slide in my pool.
I'm always smiling and as proud as can be,
That my two dads chose to provide for me.

It doesn't matter how someone's family is set,
What matters is the love and care that they get.
My family may not have a mom and a dad,
But all families are different, and that's not bad!

How lucky am I to be their son,
My dads fill my life with happiness and fun.
I count all of my blessings, it feels so nice,
When I get to dad, I count the word twice.

45

William's Way

Hi there! I'm William! "All You Need Is Love" is the story about how I was adopted and became part of a loving family. Adoption is wonderful because it not only gives a child the chance to be in a loving home, but it also helps people become parents. My family is not like most families you may see. I have two dads! When two people fall in love, it is normal for them to get married and start a family. My fathers are gay and have always wanted to get married and have children. Some people may not agree with my dads adopting me, but I couldn't be happier that they chose me to be their son.

For more learning, fun, and activities with me, check out my page on ToleranceTykes.com.

William

How Should You Treat Someone Who Has Same-Sex Parents?

• **BE KIND:** Not everyone has the same type of family as you do. Be kind and never make someone feel bad for being adopted or having same-sex parents. After all, the most important thing is that they are loved and cared for.

• **STAND UP:** If you see someone being bullied for having same-sex parents, stand up for them and let others know that bullying is not ok.

• **LEARN:** Take the time to get to know and learn about someone who has same-sex parents. Parents are there to support, guide, and love their children. It doesn't matter who the parents are or who they love.

• **TEACH:** If you or someone you know has same-sex parents, teach others how wonderful it can be. The more people who know about same-sex adoption, the more people will realize how truly great it is.

• **UNDERSTAND:** Understand that even if same-sex adoption is something that some people do not accept, it is not ok to judge. Everyone is different and no one should be able to say that it is right or wrong.

• **SUPPORT:** If you know someone who has same-sex parents or that is a same-sex parent, let them know that you support them. Having support of others makes everyday life that much better.

Homework

Let's Chat!

1) What does family mean to you?

2) Do you know anyone who has two moms or two dads?

3) How would you treat a child like William who has two dads?

Look It Up!
What percent of adopted children are raised by same-sex parents?

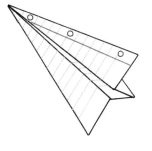

Meet Sarah

I Have A Stutter

Sarah's Speech

Hello, my name is Sarah; I brought you here to teach
About the time my teacher said I had to make a speech.
I always do my homework; I pass each and every test,
She even said my writing skills were better than the best.

The speech would be next Friday at the school's third-grade fair,
Teachers, friends, and parents would sure enough be there.
I know it's a great honor, and I should be filled with pride,
But the thought of speaking on a stage makes me want to hide.

I often stay real quiet; I never speak in class,
If given the chance to read aloud, I always politely pass.
I can see it now -- the gym is full, and my heart will start to flutter,
My biggest fear is coming true; they'll know I have a stutter.

My mother said I would be fine and not to be afraid,
But she's not up there speaking to the kids in the third grade.
I had to write a speech to teach the whole class about me,
My favorite food, my biggest dream, and what I want to be.

My speech was finally written, I was prouder than could be,
My class will finally hear the words hiding inside of me.
The stage had a microphone and one bright shinning light,
I slowly walked up all the stairs and held my speech real tight.

Before I started speaking, I looked across the crowd,
At all the smiling faces to watch me read aloud.
One by one, I read each line, until I reached the last,
I told the story of exactly why I'm the quiet girl in class.

I told them that I stutter, I said it with great pride,
I'm scared to speak in front of class, even though I've tried.
My speech was finally over, and boy, did they cheer loud!
Every person then stood up, as I looked out to the crowd.

Miss Brooke hugged me tightly, and told me she was proud,
She told me not to hide my voice, and always speak out loud.
When I got to school on Monday, I was happy as could be,
Now I talk to everyone and everyone talks to me.

Sarah Says

I am so happy to meet you! I'm Sarah! "Sarah's Speech" is about me and my stutter. A stutter is a break in my speaking pattern, known as a block. Blocks make it hard for me to speak in front of people. I stutter because the blocks cause me to repeat certain sounds, syllables, and words that I use every day. My brain sends signals to the muscles I use to speak. Sometimes my brain works faster than the muscles and I begin to stutter. Stuttering can make it really hard to speak in front of large groups or even in class. It is important to be nice and understand that a stutter is not something to make fun of. For more learning, fun, and activities with me, check out my page on ToleranceTykes.com.

Sarah

How Should You Treat Someone Who Has A Stutter?

• **BE KIND:** Speaking in front of large groups can be hard for anyone. Having a stutter is not something many people can control, and being nervous can cause someone to stutter more. Always be kind and respectful to others when they speak no matter what.

• **STAND UP:** If you see someone you know being bullied because they have a stutter, stand up for them and let other people know that it is not ok to bully anyone that may be different than you.

• **LEARN:** Get to know someone who has a stutter and learn what you can do to help make them more comfortable speaking in front of people.

• **TEACH:** If you or someone you know has a stutter, teach others what you know. The more people that know what a stutter is, the less likely people will bully or judge someone who deals with it every day.

• **UNDERSTAND:** Having a stutter can be hard, especially when it comes to speaking in school or with people you don't know. It is important to understand and remember not to correct someone's speech when they begin to stutter.

• **SUPPORT:** If you know someone with a stutter, like Sarah, remember that stuttering can make communicating with people hard. Be patient with everyone and know that it is important for everyone's voice to be heard.

Homework

Let's Chat!

1) Do you know anyone with a stutter?

2) How can you help someone with a stutter become more comfortable speaking?

3) How do you think Sarah feels at the end of the story?

Look It Up!
Can you find a famous celebrity with a stutter?

Meet Zane

I Am Blind

Dog's Best Friend

Hello there, friends! My name is Zane.

I speed read braille and walk with a cane.

I'm not able to see, I'm legally blind.

I'm different than you, please be kind.

My grandpa was blind, he passed it to me.

A genetic disorder is why I can't see.

The light doesn't pass through my retina or lens,

And my brain doesn't get the signals it sends.

By my side is my service dog, Jack.

He guides me along and has my back.

He joins me at school and for walks in the park,

He's trained so well, you wont hear him bark.

Speaking of school, mine is the best.

My teacher always puts braille on my test.

My friends in class are all unique too,

We support each other, that's what friends do.

We are all different in our own special ways,

As different as different can be.

But our love and support is always there,

That's something you feel and not see.

Zane's A-Z

Hi, everyone! My name is Zane and I am blind. "Dog's Best Friend" is a story about me being blind. Being blind means that I am not able to see. Eyes are made up of many parts that all work together to help you see. The cornea, the iris, the lens, and the retina all work together to send images to your brain. Many people who are blind have seeing eye dogs like Jack. I rely on Jack, my cane, and my other senses to get around each day. I also like audio books and braille when I'm learning new things.

For more learning, activities, and fun, check out my page on ToleranceTykes.com.

How Should You Treat Someone Who Is Blind?

• **BE KIND:** Being kind to someone who does not have one or more of their senses, like vision, is so important because it lets them know that you don't think any less of them because of their disability.

• **STAND UP:** If you see someone you know being bullied because they are blind, stand up for them and let others know that it is not ok to bully someone who may be different than you.

• **LEARN:** Get to know someone who is blind, and learn what it Is like to be them. Ask questions and learn what you can do to help anyone who is not able to see. You'll be able to help others understand and make a new friend at the same time.

• **TEACH:** If you or someone you know is blind, teach others what it's like so they can understand and be helpful. The more people who know what it's like to be blind, the less bullying we will have.

• **UNDERSTAND:** It is important to understand that not everyone has all five senses. Being blind can make everyday activities difficult. Work to understand what you can do to help make being blind a little easier for someone.

• **SUPPORT:** If you know someone who is blind, like Zane, make sure they know that you support them. Everyone deserves love and support.

Homework

Let's Chat!

1) How would you treat a classmate who is blind?

2) Do you know anyone who is blind?

3) How could you help a child like Zane?

Look It Up!

Can you find a historical person who is blind?

Thanks for visiting our class! We hope you had as much fun as we did! Keep a lookout for more *Tolerance Tykes!*

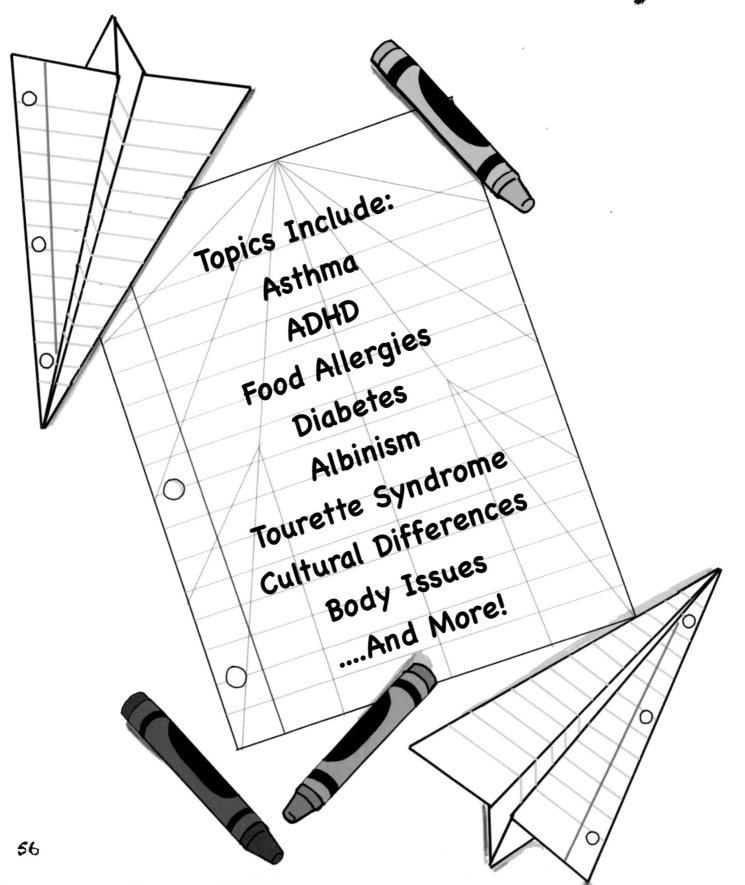

Topics Include:

Asthma

ADHD

Food Allergies

Diabetes

Albinism

Tourette Syndrome

Cultural Differences

Body Issues

....And More!

57260306R00033

Made in the USA
San Bernardino, CA
18 November 2017